Fairy Tale Adventure Crafts

Anna Llimós

Enslow Elementary
an imprint of
Enslow Publishers, Inc.
40 Industrial Road
Box 398
Berkeley Heights, NJ 07922
USA

http://www.enslow.com

C o n

Note to Kids

The materials used in this book are suggestions. If you do not have an item, use something similar. Use any color material and paint that you wish.

You can also make up a story of your own using the crafts in this book. Put on a show for your family and friends. Use your imagination!

Safety Note

Be sure to ask for help from an adult, if needed, to complete these crafts.

tents

Bubble Elf

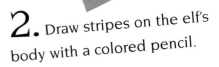

2. Draw stripes on the elf's body with a colored pencil.

1. Cut out a triangle from card stock to make the body. Cut a strip of card stock for the arms. Glue them together. Let dry.

Materials

- card stock
- clay
- colored pencils
- scissors
- white glue
- toothpick

Elf

3. Make a pair of large feet with clay. Stick the body into the feet.

4. Use a ball of clay for the head and a smaller ball for the nose. Make the eyes using two small pieces of clay. Attach the nose and eyes to the head. Draw the mouth with a toothpick.

I love blowing magic bubbles!

5. Cut out two ears from card stock and stick one into each side of the head.

6. For the hat, flatten out a piece of clay. Add clay polka dots. Cut out a triangle from the clay. Wrap the triangle around the top of the head in the shape of a cone.

Elf's House

Materials

- card stock
- corrugated paper
- clay
- toothpick
- scissors
- rolling pin
  (Ask permission first!)

3. Make a bunch of little clay balls. Add clay polka dots to the top of the mushroom.

1. Form clay into a cone shape to make the mushroom's stalk. Stick a toothpick into the top.

2. To make the top of the mushroom, make a ball of clay and flatten it on one side.

This is my mushroom house.

4. Use the toothpick to attach the top to the stalk.

5. Flatten out a piece of clay using a rolling pin. Cut out some grass from the clay with scissors. Place it around the stalk.

6. Make a chimney out of clay. Cut out a cloud of smoke from card stock. Cut out a door from corrugated paper. Attach the chimney, smoke, and door to the mushroom.

A little house for the playful elf!

7

Materials

+ card stock
+ clay
+ toothpicks
+ scissors

1. Make two balls of clay, one bigger than the other. Attach them together with a toothpick.

Frog Prince

The prince has turned into a frog!

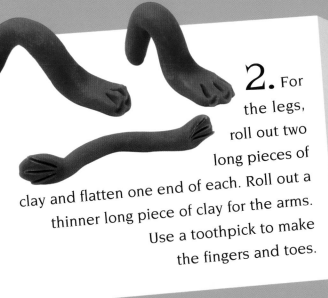

2. For the legs, roll out two long pieces of clay and flatten one end of each. Roll out a thinner long piece of clay for the arms. Use a toothpick to make the fingers and toes.

3. Attach a leg to each side of the body. Wrap the arms around the back of the head.

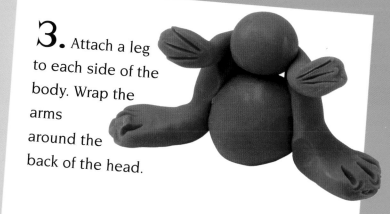

I am really a prince under a spell!

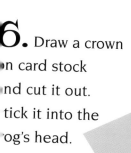

4. Use the toothpick to make the mouth and the nose. Make the eyes out of clay. Attach the eyes to the face.

6. Draw a crown on card stock and cut it out. Stick it into the frog's head.

5. Make six small balls out of clay and decorate the feet. Make three little balls of clay and decorate the belly.

9

Ogre

Materials

- thick cardboard
- clay
- tissue paper
- scissors
- glue wash (1/2 white glue, 1/2 water)
- paintbrush
- white glue
- poster paint
- stapler
- marker

3. Cover the belly and legs with pieces of tissue paper. Cover them in glue wash. Make two shoulder straps and attach them to the body with glue wash. Let dry.

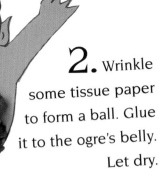

2. Wrinkle some tissue paper to form a ball. Glue it to the ogre's belly. Let dry.

1. Draw the ogre on thick cardboard with marker. Cut it out.

4. Paint the teeth and the shoes. Let dry.

I am the meanest ogre of them all!

5. Use clay to make the eyes and the nose. Glue them to the face. Let dry.

6.

Cut two strips of cardboard and fold them into triangles. Staple them closed. Glue them to the back of the ogre's body, behind the legs, so it can stand on its own.

The ogre has captured the frog prince!

1. Cut the top off the tissue box. Use a ruler to draw the four walls of the house on corrugated paper. Two walls should have triangular tops. All four walls should be the same size as the sides of the tissue box. Cut them out and glue them to the sides of the box. Let dry.

Witch's House

Materials

+ large square tissue box
+ corrugated paper
+ card stock
+ clear tape
+ scissors
+ white glue
+ ruler

The mean ogre and the poor frog arrive at the witch's house!

2. Cut out a door and a window from corrugated paper. Glue them to the front of the house. Let dry.

3. Draw grass on card stock and cut it out. Glue it around the house. Let dry.

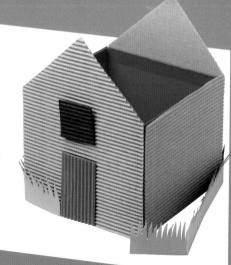

4. For the roof, cut a rectangle from corrugated paper that is a little bigger than the width of the house. Fold it in half. Cut out a small hole for the chimney. Tape the roof to the house on one side so you can open and close from the other.

5. For the chimney, roll a piece of corrugated paper into a cylinder. Glue the edge and let dry. Glue a strip of corrugated paper around the top. Let dry. Cut out a smoke cloud from card stock and stick it in the chimney. Put the chimney through the hole in the roof.

The ogre has brought me a present!

13

1. Cut out two cups from an egg carton. Paint them any color you wish. Let dry. Decorate them any way you wish with poster paint or colored pencils. Let dry.

Materials

- egg carton cups
- card stock
- colored pencils
- poster paint
- clay
- paintbrush
- toothpicks
- scissors
- white glue
- yarn

2. Stick a toothpick through one of the cups. Stick a piece of clay on top of the cup. Place the other cup over the clay and through the toothpick.

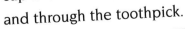

4. Make the witch's head out of clay. Mold smaller pieces of clay into two eyes and a big nose. Attach the eyes and nose to the head.

3. For the hat, cut out half a circle from card stock and decorate it with colored pencils. Roll it into the shape of a cone. Cut a long strip of card stock for the arms. Decorate it with colored pencils. Pass it through the toothpick.

Witch

The witch wants frog soup!

What tasty frog soup I am going to make!

5. Put a small piece of clay on the nose for the wart. Draw the mouth with a toothpick. Stick the head onto the tip of the toothpick.

6. Tie pieces of yarn together to make hair. Glue the yarn to the head. Let dry. Place the hat on the head.

15

Fairy Princess

Materials

- card stock
- tissue paper
- yarn
- craft wire
- glue wash (1/2 white glue, 1/2 water)
- clay
- marker
- scissors
- white glue
- tape

4. Cut ou
a circle from
card stock and
draw two eyes, a
nose, and a mouth with
a marker. Glue the head
to the dress. Let dry.

3. Twist some pieces of different colored tissue paper together at one end and tape it. This is the fairy princess's dress.

1. Twist some craft wire into wings, leaving a long stem.

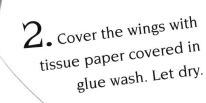

2. Cover the wings with tissue paper covered in glue wash. Let dry.

5. Tie long pieces of yarn together for the hair. Glue the hair to the head. Let dry.

6. Mix different colors of clay together to create a rock. Stick the wings in the rock. Tape the fairy princess underneath the wings.

The fairy princess rescues the frog!

Wise Tree

The tree saves the frog prince from being captured!

1. Mix different colors of clay together. Cover the paper towel tube in clay. This is the trunk.

Materials

✦ paper towel tube
✦ drinking straws
✦ card stock
✦ clay
✦ marker
✦ scissors

2. Cut some drinking straws into pieces of different lengths. Cover them with clay. Attach them to the trunk to form the branches.

3. Make the mouth by attaching two small pieces of clay to the trunk.

4. Make a nose, eyebrows, and eyes out of clay. Attach the nose, eyebrows, and eyes to the trunk.

5. Draw leaves on card stock with marker and cut them out.

6. Stick the leaves in the branches of the tree.

You will not escape!

19

1. Make the body and the arms out of clay. Attach the arms to the body with toothpicks.

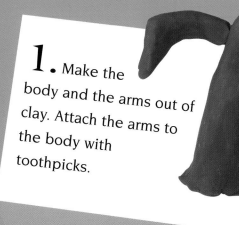

Materials

- clay
- yarn
- toothpicks
- scissors
- white glue
- rolling pin
  (Ask permission first!)

2. Add clay polka dots of different colors to the wizard's robe.

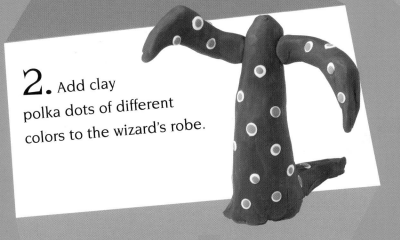

4.
Attach the head to the body with a toothpick. Tie some yarn together to make hair. Glue the yarn to the head. Let dry.

3. Make the head and the hands out of clay. Use a toothpick to make the fingers. Use small balls of clay for the eyes. Attach the eyes to the head. Attach the hands to the arms.

Wizard

Phooey! They stole the frog!

The wizard has a potion that can turn the frog back into a prince!

5. Tie short pieces of yarn together for the mustache and beard. Glue them to the face. Let dry. Make a clay nose and attach it to the face.

6. For the hat, use a rolling pin to flatten out a piece of clay into a circle. Cut the circle in half. Add clay polka dots. Wrap the half circle around the wizard's head in the shape of a cone.

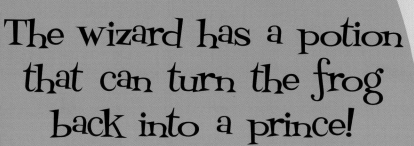

Magic Cauldron

Hocus pocus!

Materials

* clay
* dowel
* paper garland
* scissors

3. To make the spoon, stick a piece of black clay onto each end of the dowel and shape them.

1. Mix different colors of clay together. Roll out a long thin piece, coiling it around itself to form the bottom of the cauldron.

2. Roll out another long thin piece of clay. Keep coiling it around itself until the cauldron is finished.

5. For the fire, twist different colors of paper garland together. Place it around the bottom of the cauldron. Stick the spoon and a piece of garland inside the cauldron.

4. Add a thin piece of clay underneath the handle and one above the spoon.

The prince pops out of the cauldron soaking wet!

Sea Dragon

Materials

* card stock
* clay
* plastic knife
* scissors
* pencil

1. Make a ball out of different colors of clay.

2. Roll the ball out into a long, thin shape with a point on one end.

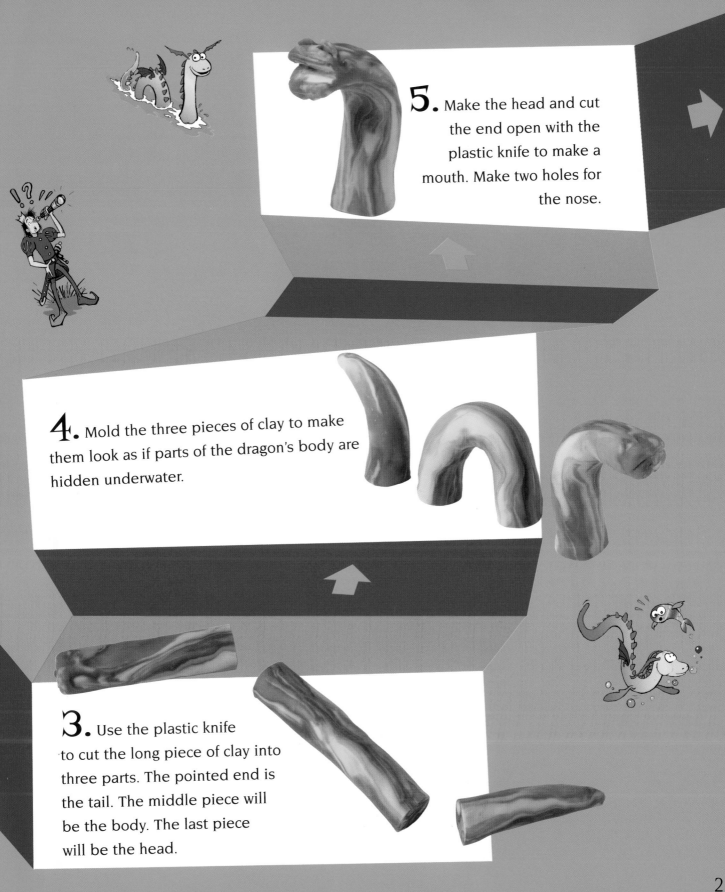

5. Make the head and cut the end open with the plastic knife to make a mouth. Make two holes for the nose.

4. Mold the three pieces of clay to make them look as if parts of the dragon's body are hidden underwater.

3. Use the plastic knife to cut the long piece of clay into three parts. The pointed end is the tail. The middle piece will be the body. The last piece will be the head.

6. Cut out many small triangles from card stock. Stick them along the dragon's back.

The prince soars on the back of his mighty sea dragon!

7. Use clay to make the eyes. Attach the eyes to the head.

8. Draw two ears on card stock and cut them out.

9. Stick an ear into each side of the dragon's head.

10. Draw a pair of wings on card stock and cut them out. Stick one wing into each side of the body.

Create your own story with all the crafts in this book!

There was once . . .

an elf in the
magic forest.

One day, he saw a frog
prince jump around.

He trapped the frog
inside one of his bubbles to save him.

But the ogre popped the
bubble and took the frog.

The ogre took
the frog to the
witch's house.

The witch wanted to
make frog soup.

But the fairy princess saved the frog prince.

The wise tree stopped the witch and the ogre from chasing the fairy princess.

The fairy princess and the frog went to see the wizard.

The wizard threw the frog into the cauldron and . . . Surprise! A brave prince popped out!

The prince and his flying dragon left the magic forest and returned to his kingdom.

The end.

Enslow Elementary, an imprint of Enslow Publishers, Inc.
Enslow Elementary® is a registered trademark of Enslow Publishers, Inc.

Translated from the Spanish edition by Stacey Juana Pontoriero.
Edited and produced by Enslow Publishers, Inc.

Library-in-Cataloging Publication Data

Llimós Plomer, Anna.
[Crea tu. Bosque mágico. English]
Fairy tale adventure crafts / Anna Llimós.
p. cm. — (Fun adventure crafts)
Includes bibliographical references and index.
Summary: "Provides step-by-step instructions on how to make eleven
simple fairy-tale-themed crafts, such as an ogre, wizard, fairy princess,
and more, and it includes a story for kids to tell with their crafts"—
Provided by publisher.
ISBN 978-0-7660-3736-6
1. Handicraft—Juvenile literature. 2. Fairy tales in art—Juvenile
literature. I. Title. II. Title: Bosque mágico.
TT160.L57513 2010
745.5—dc22
                              2009041477
ISBN-13: 978-0-7660-3737-3 (paperback ed.)

Originally published in Spanish under the title *Crea tu . . . Bosque
mágico.*
Copyright © 2007 PARRAMÓN EDICIONES, S.A., - World Rights.
Published by Parramón Ediciones, S.A., Barcelona, Spain.
Text and exercises: Anna Llimós
Illustrator: Àlex Sagarra
Photographs: Nos & Soto

Printed in Spain

122009 Gráficas 94 S.L., Barcelona, Spain

10 9 8 7 6 5 4 3 2 1

To Our Readers: We have done our best to make sure all
Internet Addresses in this book were active and appropriate
when we went to press. However, the author and the publishers have no control over and assume no liability for the
material available on those Internet sites or on other Web
sites they may link to. Any comments or suggestions can be
sent by e-mail to comments@enslow.com or to the address
on the back cover.

Read About

Books

Ross, Kathy. *Fairy World Crafts.*
Minneapolis, Minn.: Millbrook Press,
2008.

Sadler, Judy Ann. *The New Jumbo Book
of Easy Crafts.* Toronto: Kids Can Press,
2009.

Internet Addresses

Fairy Princess Craft, DLTK's Crafts for Kids
<http://www.dltk-kids.com/crafts/birthday/
mfairyprincess.html>

Magic Wand Craft, DLTK's Crafts for Kids
<http://www.dltk-kids.com/fantasy/
wand.htm>

Index